MW00512570

*And you show that you are
a letter from Christ delivered by us,
written not with ink but with the Spirit
of the living God, not on tablets of stone
but on tablets of human hearts.*

2 CORINTHIANS 3:3

Celebrate Salvation!®

Sent
Becoming a Living Letter

Stage C - Sharing the Good News of God's Kingdom

The Joy of Christian Discipleship Series
Book 3

Dr. Bill Morehouse

His Kingdom Press

About Dr. Bill Morehouse

Dr. Morehouse was raised in a traditional Christian home in the 1950's and functionally became a humanist during college and medical school in the 1960's. After completing his medical residency in Family Medicine in the early 1970's he embarked on a career of serving the poor but soon found that his secular faith and alternative lifestyle were woefully inadequate to the task.

In 1974 he underwent a dramatic conversion from the philosophy and lifestyle he had been living to a wholehearted commitment to Jesus as his LORD and Savior. After returning to medicine and marrying in 1975, he and his wife dedicated themselves to growing in faith, raising their family of four children (plus spouses and grandchildren), and providing Christ-centered service to some of the most disadvantaged members of their community.

Since retiring from active clinical practice in July 2018, Dr. Morehouse has devoted himself to continued Christian growth, study, writing, and teaching about the Kingdom of God. He has had long personal and professional experience with the material covered in Celebrate Salvation.®

Sent: Becoming a Living Letter
Copyright 2020 by William R. Morehouse
ISBN: 978-1-7353899-3-6 (paperback)
Web Address: www.celebratesalvation.org

 His Kingdom Press
Rochester, New York 14619

Special discounts are available on quantity purchases by corporations, associations, educators, and others. For details, contact the publisher through www.hiskingdom.us/press.

Sent Contents

Background Material

Meeting 21ˢᵗ Century Needs 1

The Joy of Christian Discipleship Course 1 3
Established in 3 Stages and 7 Steps

Group Guidelines 5

Confession and Prayer 6

Sowing and Reaping 7

Sent: Becoming a Living Letter

Stage C - Sharing the Good News of God's Kingdom 9

Step 7: The Great Commission in Word
Lesson 1: The Gospel of the Kingdom 11
Lesson 2: The Kingdom in today's world 15
Lesson 3: Sharing our testimonies 19
Lesson 4: Sharing the Word of God 23

Step 7: The Great Commission in Deed
Lesson 5: Recognizing the poor 27
Lesson 6: Opportunities to share 31
Lesson 7: Demonstrating God's love 35
Lesson 8: Exercising our gifts 39

Step 7: The Great Commission in Power
Lesson 9: Natural and supernatural 43
Lesson 10: Seeking God for the afflicted 47
Lesson 11: Salvation and healing 51
Lesson 12: Imparting the gifts 55

Suggestions for Further Study 60

Acknowledgements

The work you have in your hands is part of a collaboration with roots that extend back for generations and even millennia. Jesus came to reveal God's love to struggling mankind and to demonstrate the depth of that love in ways that have had a profound impact on countless lives ever since. He embodied the fullness of God in human form and called us out of darkness, confusion, and bondage into the wonderful light, clarity, and freedom we were created to inhabit.

We appear to start out so fresh and pure as infants but soon become soiled and spoiled. Then as the years go by we get deeper and deeper in. As the Psalmist wrote:

The LORD looks down from heaven on the children of man, to see if there are any who understand, who seek after God. They have all turned aside; together they have become corrupt; there is none who does good, not even one.

Psalm 14:2-3, also noted in Psalm 53:1-3 and Romans 3:10-12

How can we come clean? Do you believe in second, third, and even seven times seventieth chances? God does.

Historically, there were entire eras when certain troubling human conditions, like addictions and criminal behavior, were just written off as hopeless. This work owes a deep debt of ongoing gratitude, first to the God who saves and then to fellow believers in the Body of Christ who are working tirelessly to reveal and share the truth that God hears our prayers and has life-giving answers for even our most challenging and "unsolvable" problems.

Many people are continuing to contribute their prayers, thoughts, ideas, and constructive comments to the growth and development of Celebrate Salvation.® I am particularly grateful for the pioneering work of John Baker, Rick Warren, and their colleagues at Saddleback Church as well as to many contributors in my local church fellowship and beyond. I would especially like to honor my wife and life partner, Susan, for her unfailing love and support over the decades we have been given to share life, faith, family, and community together.

Meeting 21ˢᵗ Century Needs

Celebrate Salvation® has developed a broad-based Christ-centered study series and discipleship program designed to reach a wide audience of sincere seekers. Are you searching for truth in our troubled age, a new believer seeking to be grounded, someone who has recently renewed your faith commitment in Christ and wants to revitalize your faith and ability to be an effective witness to others, or a church leader committed to growth? If so, this course is for you.

Celebrate Salvation's® underlying design is based on a set of several Biblical understandings first clearly outlined during the Oxford Group revival in the early 20ᵗʰ Century. One outgrowth of this movement became the time-honored 12-Steps and Traditions of Alcoholics Anonymous which have been instrumental in helping millions find God-given strength to overcome addictive behaviors. However, since then many 12-step recovery programs have revised their terminology to reach people who've had negative experiences with organized religion by replacing references to "God" with the term "a higher power" which is left up to each participant to define.

In the 1990s the 12-Step approach was significantly reframed by John Baker and Rick Warren at Saddleback Church into a clearly Christian program compatible with its Oxford Group roots. Following the original understandings, they condensed the 12 Steps of Anonymous programs back down to 8 Principles or Choices coupled with Bible references. Since then millions more have followed their highly-successful Celebrate Recovery® (CR) program to find freedom in Christ and victory over a wide array of common human difficulties.

Over the years, many have observed that Step programs capture the essential and lifelong Biblical dynamics involved in becoming a spiritually born again believer and active disciple of Jesus Christ. 12-Step programs may hold meetings in houses of worship but choose to operate independently of religion. On the other hand, CR was designed to be sponsored by local churches as an outreach ministry with a focus on people who self-identify as needing recovery from a number of challenging life situations, including addictions. In any given area there also may or may not be an active CR presence, a situation that calls for a discipleship program with a wider reach and deeper integration with the core mission of the church.

Sadly, struggles with pornography and other negative or destructive attitudes or behaviors that impair a Christian's walk with Christ are not generally covered in pulpit messages or new member classes for a number of reasons. Perhaps it's because people may be reluctant to be open about potentially embarrassing problems or individual home fellowship groups or congregations may lack the capacity to handle them. Access to Christian growth and discipleship resources for helping members and new believers overcome personal issues and become solidly rooted in their faith may also be limited.

Now in the 21st century we are again facing widespread social changes that are challenging the moral and spiritual roots of our civilization. As the prophet said,

Justice is turned back, and righteousness stands far away; for truth has stumbled in the public squares, and uprightness cannot enter. Isaiah 59:14

Many of us find ourselves aching for an outpouring of God's Holy Spirit, for times of widespread revival and spiritual awakening. Are we prepared? What would happen if God were to answer our prayers and pour out His Spirit throughout our communities, breaking open those already in the church and bringing in a large influx of new believers laden with the issues of our modern world? Would we and our churches know how to handle an Awakening like this?

Celebrate Salvation® has taken the Oxford Group's understandings, as modified by 12-Step and CR programs, and clarified them further with grateful credit to make them available to the church at large.

Discovering the ever-unfolding mystery of faith in the living God is a wonderfully profound, life-changing, and satisfying gift. Our hope is that this modest series of introductory studies will provide a Biblically balanced and sound foundation for the faith which is widely applicable, reproducible, and fruitful. Please use the materials in *The Joy of Christian Discipleship Series* and augment them with those of your own fellowship group as we seek to meet the needs of our time with God's faithful Word.

Dr. Bill Morehouse
October 2020

Meeting 21st Century Needs

Celebrate Salvation!®
The Joy of Christian Discipleship Course 1
Established in 3 Stages and 7 Steps

Saved! Rescued by Grace
A – Foundational Principles of the Good News

1. **Recognize the trouble I'm in:** Admit that I'm dealing with issues that are beyond my control and need help getting and keeping my life on the right track.

2. **Believe in God's love:** Believe that God is really in charge, loves me, and earnestly desires to exercise His Kingdom power to rescue me and work it all out.

3. **Let go and let God:** Consciously choose to commit all my life and will to Jesus Christ's care and control.

Sanctified: Coming Clean with God
B – Living in the Word and the World

4. **Conviction and Repentance:** Evaluate my life and all my relationships in the light of the Holy Spirit and then openly confess my faults to myself, to God, and to others that I trust. Forgive those who have hurt me and seek restitution and reconciliation wherever possible.

5. **Trust and Obey:** Voluntarily submit to any and all changes God wants to make in my life and humbly ask Him to cleanse me and progressively remove all my character defects.

6. **Communicating with God:** Reserve dedicated time with God for self-examination, Bible reading, fasting and prayer in order to know God and His will for my life and to gain the power to follow His will.

Sent: Becoming a Living Letter
C – Sharing the Good News of God's Kingdom

7. **The Great Commission:** Celebrate the joy of my salvation by following God's lead in bringing His Good News to others in word, deed, and power.

Background Material

About Course 1

The material in **Course 1** of *The Joy of Christian Discipleship Series* has been developed in the form of three books, 1-3, one for each foundational Stage of Christian discipleship with significant expansion on the Great Commission in the third. These workbooks are designed to serve as study guides for small discipleship groups of 2-12 (ideal 3-8) committed members. Each of the three studies can be completed in about 12 weekly group sessions over one semester or 3-month period with breaks for holidays.

New groups may gather and start at any time with mature leaders who have already gone through the material themselves or have been raised up in similar 12-Step and/or CR programs in other settings. A good way for congregations to get a Celebrate Salvation® course going in their church is to gather current members together who have had some experience in discipleship or recovery groups and embark on a planning process for reviewing and introducing the study series into the life of their fellowship. It's not only wise but essential to plan on organizing separate groups for men and women, given the personal nature of discipleship and the relationships that develop, including those between leaders and members newer in the faith.

Each of the three guides in **Course 1** is divided into twelve 4-page weekly lessons containing four lessons on each of the three Steps in the first two guides and four lessons on carrying out the Great Commission in Word, Deed, and Power in the third. Supplementary handouts and worksheets designed to accompany each book in the series are available in a companion book or online at www.celebratesalvation.org/more.

This third guide is entitled *"Sent: Becoming a Living Letter"* and covers what it means to continue the ongoing cycle of cleansing and growing in faith as we carry out the Great Commission in accordance with God's Word.

> *"Go into all the world and proclaim the gospel to the whole creation. Whoever believes and is baptized will be saved, but whoever does not believe will be condemned."*
> Mark 16:15-16

Discipleship Course Design

Group Guidelines

1. Prepare for each meeting by reading the week's lesson and writing out your answers to the questions in advance.
2. Please keep your group sharing focused on your own thoughts, feelings, experiences, and insights about each question. Limit your sharing to allow others time to share.
3. Try to avoid cross-talk. Cross-talk is when people interrupt or engage in side conversations that exclude others. Each person should be free to express their own feelings without interruptions.
4. We are here to support one another, not to instruct, preach at, or "fix" one another.
5. Anonymity and confidentiality are essential requirements in a trusting discipleship group. Personal information that is shared in the group stays in the group unless permission is given or someone threatens to injure themselves or others.
6. Offensive or demeaning language is unwelcome in any Christian fellowship group.
7. Please silence your personal electronic devices and put them away. Recording during meetings is prohibited.

Suggestions for Group Leadership

Organize separate groups for men and women to ensure safe, open sharing. Schedule regular weekly meetings to last about 90 minutes. Make sure all participants have study guides and access to handouts.

1. Gather group in a circle and open meeting on time with prayer and brief comments about group business and upcoming events.
2. Go around circle with introductions including first name, brief confession of faith, and primary issues for personal growth.
3. Continue around circle by reading 3 Stages and 7 Steps, followed by Group Guidelines and then, in unison, one of the Confessional Prayers.
4. Start each lesson by reading the introductory paragraphs around the circle and then opening with the first question.
5. Keep one-by-one sharing going around the circle within Guidelines.
6. Circulate basket for prayer requests; then recirculate so each person who submitted one can take a different one home for intercession.
7. Bring copies of next week's handouts for those who need them.
8. Close meeting on time with prayer, allowing members to linger for conversation for a while. Refreshments optional.

Background Material

Confession and Prayer

The 23rd Psalm

The LORD is my shepherd; I shall not want. He makes me lie down in green pastures. He leads me beside still waters. He restores my soul. He leads me in paths of righteousness for his name's sake. Even though I walk through the valley of the shadow of death, I will fear no evil, for you are with me; your rod and your staff, they comfort me. You prepare a table before me in the presence of my enemies; you anoint my head with oil; my cup overflows. Surely goodness and mercy shall follow me all the days of my life, and I shall dwell in the house of the LORD forever.

David

The LORD's Prayer

"Our Father in heaven, hallowed be Your Name. Your Kingdom come, Your will be done on earth as it is in heaven. Give us this day our daily bread, and forgive us our debts, as we forgive our debtors. Do not lead us into temptation, but deliver us from the evil one, for Yours is the Kingdom and the power and the glory forever. Amen."

Jesus

The Serenity Prayer

God, grant me the serenity to accept the things I cannot change, the courage to change the things I can, and the wisdom to know the difference. Living one day at a time, enjoying one moment at a time; accepting hardship as a pathway to peace; taking, as Jesus did, this sinful world as it is, not as I would have it; trusting that You will make all things right if I surrender to Your will; so that I may be reasonably happy in this life and supremely happy with You forever in the next. Amen.

Reinhold Niebuhr

Prayer

Sowing and Reaping

In the famous Broadway musical "The Fantasticks" neighboring fathers Bellomy and Hucklebee sing the song "Plant a Radish" about how different children are from plants that goes like this:

Plant a radish. Get a radish. Never any doubt.
That's why I love vegetables; you know what you're about!

With human beings we often get what we sow, however, without being quite aware of what we're sowing. Are they picking up on our good behavior, habits, and words or on our more damaged traits? To take the analogy further, consider education. We hope that the teachers, reading, studies, and experiences we devote ourselves and our children to will add value to our lives. Using the computer analogy we gave in our study guide on Sanctification, whatever we take in becomes part of the programming and data that we operate on.

The sowing and reaping analogy, however, presents the image of a farmer's field. What kind of crop will it grow? Of course, that depends to a large extent on how carefully the ground has been prepared and the soil tilled as well as on the choice of seed, irrigation, and weeding. One of the more well-known parables that Jesus taught was about the sower and the seed in Matthew 13. You might enjoy taking time to read it now.

Jesus explains in this parable that the good seed is the Word of God and the soil is the hearts of men and women. Has the soil been prepared or is it hard and rocky?

Just for a moment, let's consider our own hearts. Are there still hard and rocky places in them? Are we sowing good seed into them that will stay, grow, and produce more seed that we can cast into the hearts of others along our way in life? That's what we're being sanctified for, to be sent into the world as tillers and sowers of the living Word of God.

How do we know that we have what it takes to be useful in God's Kingdom in this way? Our souls were hardened by sin. Rocks and bad seed had been scattered in them, often with our full cooperation, by an enemy of our souls. The good seed had been left in old Bibles on the shelf. The answer to our question lies hidden in an ancient instruction given by the prophet Hosea;

Sow for yourselves righteousness; reap steadfast love; break up your fallow ground, for it is the time to seek the LORD, that he may come and rain righteousness upon you.
Hosea 10:12

The key is "fallow ground" (just one word רִיב in Hebrew). Fallow ground refers to soil that's been left alone for a while to settle before being replanted. God knows the field is good for growing a crop: it just has to be cleared, plowed up, and tilled before it will hold the good seed and bear a harvest.

You are one of those good fields, chosen and being prepared by the Master for a good harvest! Don't lose heart during the preparation phase. It's like you've been accepted into medical school and are enrolled in classes. You're going to make a great doctor: just hang in there and study to show yourself approved. Cooperate as He breaks up your fallow ground and sows the seed of the Word of God in the fresh furrows. Help Him along the way. Water and weed.

Let us not grow weary of doing good, for in due season we will reap, if we do not give up.
Galatians 6:9

And I am sure of this, that he who began a good work in you will bring it to completion at the day of Jesus Christ.
Philippians 1:6

Just yield to the One who plows and tills, open your hearts wide to His Word, and be prepared for a harvest, first in your own life and family and then in the community around you. Do you want a big harvest?

Remember this: Whoever sows sparingly will also reap sparingly, and whoever sows generously will also reap generously.
2 Corinthians 9:6

Are you ready? Let's go for it!

Sent: Becoming a Living Letter
Sharing the Good News of God's Kingdom

Step 7: The Great Commission: Celebrate the joy of my salvation by following God's lead in bringing His Good News to others in word, deed, and power.

But you are a chosen race, a royal priesthood, a holy nation, a people for his own possession, that you may proclaim the excellencies of him who called you out of darkness into his marvelous light.

1 Peter 2:9

What is a dream? We've all had them while we're sleeping, and even puppy dogs and babies seem to dream, judging by their facial expressions and limb movements.

But what about during the day when we're awake? Do we dream then? Yes, we do, but often we don't tap into our dreams even though, broken or not, they guide us. Let's open a window into this realm by asking the question this way: what are the dreams on your heart or, in other words, what's the condition of your hopes for the future?

We can list our short-term hopes rather easily and some longer term aspirations and goals, but what about something larger? What would you like the future to look like for you and your family and perhaps even beyond for your neighborhood, community, and world? What are your hopes, visions and dreams, including things that are beyond your direct influence? What would you like to see improved? Are there good dreams out there for making life and the world of humanity better that you can tap into and become part of?

This kind of thinking gets us into the realm of broader visions like the "American dream" and the Kingdom of God. Egypt's Pharaoh had a dream and so did Moses. The Philistines had a dream and so did King David. Julius Caesar had a dream and so did Jesus of Nazareth. Constantine had dreams and so did Saint Augustine and Muhammad. Thomas Jefferson and Karl Marx had dreams and so did Martin Luther and Gandhi. Even Hitler dreamed of a glorious (but hideous) Third Reich, and more recently MLK, Jr. shared a compelling dream.

Our world has been filled with dreams of all descriptions. We also have our broken dreams and nightmares, but we keep returning, pressing into hope and prayer, trusting that somewhere, under or over the rainbow, things will get better. What are the politicians and faith leaders of today dreaming? What is your dream? And are any of the hopes we're carrying based on the reality of what our eternal and loving God has for us?

Into this human realm of desire and hope in the midst of the world's chaos and brokenness we discover that a most unusual man, Jesus, has brought a message that he says is Good News from his Father, the very God of the universe. A simple version goes like this: "My Father loves all of you, is ready to forgive you, and wants you to be part of His Kingdom of love and forgiveness and joy and peace and goodness in this present world and into eternity. Are you interested?"

People often dismiss the Good News (or Gospel) that Jesus brought because, to put it simply, it not only sounds "too good to be true" but gets ruled out when you hear the price: your entire life. It's worth the sacrifice, Jesus says, because you're going to have to give that up when you die anyway. What?? This man must either be insane or actually telling the truth. For those of us who have said "yes" He has not only proved His sanity but given us the testimony of a new life in His Kingdom.

The Good News that we carry appeals first to the humble who recognize their need for help. It's most difficult for the proud who think they know it all. When shared with an understanding of the Word of God and empathy for people's needs, demonstrated by deeds that are guided by the King of Kings, and backed up by the power of His Holy Spirit, the Gospel of the Kingdom is real and irresistible. Let's become living letters who bring God's Good News wherever we go!

For the love of Christ controls us... that those who live might no longer live for themselves but for him who for their sake died and was raised.

2 Corinthians 5:14-15

Sharing the Good News

Lesson 1C
The Gospel of the Kingdom

Step 7: The Great Commission: Celebrate the joy of my salvation by following God's lead in bringing His Good News to others in **word**, deed, and power.

Learning about and understanding the Good News or Gospel of the Kingdom.

To Him who loves us and has freed us from our sins by His blood and made us a kingdom, priests to His God and Father, to Him be glory and dominion forever and ever. Amen. Revelation 1:5-6

The original text of the New Testament used the Greek word εὐαγγέλιον (*euangelion*), translated as "gospel" to identify the message that Jesus brought. Most of us understand that this word means "good news" of a very special kind having to do with Jesus and God the Father's relationship with mankind.

For many people the message of the Gospel of Jesus boils down to this: Jesus came to announce forgiveness of sins, salvation from eternal damnation, and the free gift of eternal life after death to all who would believe in Him. Although the elements of this are true, there is much more to the story. After Jesus had been baptized, emerged victorious from 40 days of being tempted by the devil in the wilderness, and was in the process of calling His first 12 disciples, Matthew records the following:

*From that time Jesus began to preach, saying, "Repent, for the **kingdom of heaven** is at hand"... And he went throughout all Galilee, teaching in their synagogues and proclaiming the **gospel of the kingdom** and healing every disease and every affliction among the people.* Matthew 4:17, 23

A brief word study will lead us to discover that *euangelion* in this passage and all others where "gospel" is mentioned actually means a special kind of "good news" – the announcement of the appearance or

Sent: Becoming a Living Letter

accession to the throne of a mighty ruler. In the Greek language of the time it denoted a weighty, authoritative, royal, and official message.

Taken in the context that Jesus always used it, the "gospel of the kingdom of heaven (or God)" was an official announcement in word, deed, and power of His arrival as the King of Kings, the Messiah and Lord of all. This was "good news" indeed, but the news had to do with the emergence of the Kingdom of God on earth in all its glory and power. The God of the universe is here and available to demonstrate His comfort, love, forgiveness, healing, and victory over death – right now!

God's in charge around here, and you and I can join together with Him in addressing and working toward resolving not only our afflictions but those of this troubled world in which we live. He lives forever, and so can we if we will only let go of our human control and let Him take charge of our lives.

The older and more wearied we get of proud human fallibility and the false hopes it offers, the more palpable this "Good News" becomes. We can cease from our own striving, rest in the King's personal leadership, and turn ourselves with all our hopes and expectations over to Him who died for us. Then He is able to use us in His Kingdom in the here and now.

My Experiences of Sharing God's Word

1. How did you come to Christ? Who shared with you, and what was their message?

2. Have you tried sharing "The Gospel" with anyone? What message did you share, and what results did you have?

3. Can you see the Kingdom of God at work in our world right now? How can you be part of it?

4. What does it mean to you to turn the authority of your life over to a King you can't see? How can you do it daily?

14

5. Who do you care about that you would like to be able to share the Gospel of the Kingdom with? Make a prayer list below.

Be thorough while you're answering each question by taking additional notes on sheets of paper or in an ongoing daily journal of your insights, meditations, prayers, and thoughts.

You might also appreciate our **Good News in the Lord's Prayer** handout at www.celebratesalvation.org/more. This is a good time to start or go deeper into your own Bible study of "the Gospel of the Kingdom" in the four Gospel accounts.

Memorizing Scripture

As discussed in the preceding Study Guide, an excellent spiritual discipline to develop as you grow as a disciple is memorizing Scripture. Notice that we've suggested a number of short Scripture passages for memorization in the Study Guides by printing them in blue. Each one is pertinent to the lessons being covered.

This Lesson started with a suggested passage from Revelation 1. It always helps to understand the context of what you're committing to memory, so try to look up each passage and read the verses that precede and follow it, then repeat the passage several times to capture it in your memory bank. Repeat it again for review later on, and it will be yours!

Lesson 2C
The Kingdom in today's world

Step 7: The Great Commission: Celebrate the joy of my salvation by following God's lead in bringing His Good News to others in **word**, deed, and power.

What, where, and how does the Kingdom of God (or "the heavens") interact with our lives in today's world?

"The hour is coming, and is now here, when the true worshipers will worship the Father in spirit and truth, for the Father is seeking such people to worship him. God is spirit, and those who worship him must worship in spirit and truth."
John 4:23-24

The God who created the universe exists in a realm that is beyond our imaginations, outside but containing the confines of time and space in the worlds we can see. He can be appreciated in two ways: naturally by observing His works and spiritually by discerning His presence and the power of His Word.

When I look at your heavens, the work of your fingers, the moon and the stars, which you have set in place, what is man that you are mindful of him, and the son of man that you care for him?
Psalm 8:3-4

"The wind blows where it wishes, and you hear its sound, but you do not know where it comes from or where it goes. So it is with everyone who is born of the Spirit."
John 3:8

There is an old theory that God is like a watchmaker who created a universe with natural laws and then left it to run on its own without any further involvement. It would be difficult for anyone who has come this far in our Celebrate Salvation® series to agree that the loving God who sent His only begotten Son to redeem us is not intimately caring and mindful in human affairs.

As we experience His loving presence and grow in faith and our knowledge of His Word, we begin to see more and more how His amazing grace has been active in our midst ever since He made the

Sent: Becoming a Living Letter

heavens and the earth. We can count on Him in everything – in our own lives and those of our family members and in our neighbors, our communities, nations, and the entire world. Along with that awareness there comes a deep joy and peace, the *shalom* peace of God that passes all understanding.

Don't you wish everyone could appreciate the love, hope, joy, and peace of our God? Let it show in the daily words of your mouth and genuine encouragement of your presence. That's what it means to let your light shine by being a Living Letter:

> *In your hearts honor Christ the Lord as holy, always being prepared to make a defense to anyone who asks you for a reason for the hope that is in you; yet do it with gentleness and respect.*
> 1 Peter 3:15

> *"Let your light shine before others, so that they may see your good works and give glory to your Father who is in heaven."*
> Matthew 5:16

The brighter the Word of God glows in our hearts, the more visible it becomes on our faces. Could it possibly be that this is what the early Christian artists were trying to depict when they drew likenesses of the "saints" (sanctified ones) with halos shining around their heads?

My Understanding of God's Kingdom

1. How do you see God working in your life now? What about your family and friends?

2. Are there any other places in the world where you've seen God at work? Where are you hoping to see Him work?

3. How well have you been able to "let go and let God" and reap the joy of "single column accounting" that goes with it?

4. Are people able to see enough hope in you to ask about where it comes from? How would or do you respond?

18

5. What are you doing now that could bear witness to God's presence and activity in your life?

6. Doctors and musicians "practice" regularly to improve their performance. Are you practicing being a Living Letter daily?

Be thorough while you're answering each question by taking additional notes on sheets of paper or in an ongoing daily journal of your insights, meditations, prayers, and thoughts.

You may also enjoy reading **God Governs in Mankind's Affairs**, our handout which contains the full text of Benjamin Franklin's 1787 Address to the Constitutional Convention on Prayer, which is posted at www.celebratesalvation.org/more.

Lesson 3C
Sharing our testimonies

Step 7: The Great Commission: Celebrate the joy of my salvation by following God's lead in bringing His Good News to others in **word**, deed, and power.

How can we effectively share His Good News through our lives and testimonies?

For I am not ashamed of the gospel, for it is the power of God for salvation to everyone who believes. Romans 1:16

The Gospel of the Kingdom is a message that God tailors to the individual needs of every person at each and every point in their life's journey. In addition to the great IAM being the Creator and Sustainer of the universe, He is the King of kings and Lord of lords, the Author and Finisher of our faith, and the Wonderful Counselor and Great Physician of mankind.

We have to remember that it's not our responsibility to "save" people – this is God's job: we're just called to come alongside Him in what He is already doing in the lives of those around us. If He's comforting, we comfort; if leading, we lead with Him. As the Apostle Paul instructed in his letter to the Roman church:

Having gifts that differ according to the grace given to us, let us use them: if prophecy, in proportion to our faith; if service, in our serving; the one who teaches, in his teaching; the one who exhorts, in his exhortation; the one who contributes, in generosity; the one who leads, with zeal; the one who does acts of mercy, with cheerfulness. Let love be genuine. Romans 12:6-12

First, a word about formulas for sharing the Gospel message:

Jesus said that the only way you can enter the Kingdom of God is to be *"born again of water and the Spirit"* (John 3.5), but our job is not to look over everyone we meet, open our obstetrical kits, pull out our formulas, and try to deliver them on the nearest bed.

Sent: Becoming a Living Letter

Spiritual obstetrics (evangelism) is a ministry with many aspects, including prenatal and postpartum care as well as actual delivery supervision. First, a person must be mature and exposed to the fertile seed of the Word of God enough to be spiritually pregnant before an assessment of spiritual pregnancy can even be made. Discernment, sensitivity, and timing are essential or people may be damaged, offended, or birthed prematurely with sad results.

Neither he who plants nor he who waters is anything, but only God who gives the growth. He who plants and he who waters are one, and each will receive his wages according to his labor. For we are God's fellow workers. You are God's field, God's building. 1 Corinthians 3:7-9

Yes, we're to be bold and not ashamed but we're also to be gentle, loving, patient, and kind. We win the hearts of others through showing the genuine love of God, sprinkling our testimonies with the Word of God like a seasoning salt, and waiting prayerfully upon Him for grace in allowing the much-misunderstood but freely available gift of "prophecy" to operate through us:

Pursue love, and earnestly desire the spiritual gifts, especially that you may prophesy… the one who prophesies speaks to people for their upbuilding and encouragement and consolation. 1 Corinthians 14:1-3

My Attempts to Share the Gospel

1. How did others share with you before you were born again into God's Kingdom? What was it that captured your heart?

2. Who among your immediate circle of family, friends, and acquaintances are you praying for? What are their needs?

3. "Friendship evangelism" recommends forming a long-term bond before sharing the Gospel. But is the bond's duration or integrity more important?

4. How many forms can the "Good News" of the Gospel of the Kingdom come in? List some below:

22

5. What are the essentials of the Gospel message that you feel equipped to share now? What more are you seeking??

Be thorough while you're answering each question by taking additional notes below as well as on additional sheets of paper or in an ongoing daily journal of your insights, meditations, prayers, and thoughts. Don't forget to memorize!

Consider reading and pondering on Charles Swindoll's famous quote about **Attitude**, available online at www.celebratesalvation.org/more.

Lesson 4C
Sharing the Word of God

Step 7: The Great Commission: Celebrate the joy of my salvation by following God's lead in bringing His Good News to others in **word**, deed, and power.

Studying, learning, memorizing, and appropriately sharing the Word of God with sensitivity.

Most of us know what it feels like to say something and either regret it later or marvel at how apt it was to the situation. At this point in our lives we earnestly want fewer instances of the former and more of the latter. As Solomon wrote:

A word fitly spoken is like apples of gold in a setting of silver.

Proverbs 25:11

The surest way to have your words bear fruit in the lives of others is to have them grounded in and molded by the plans, thoughts, and ways of the living God as revealed in His Word. When we study, learn, and store up God's Word in our hearts we make it accessible to us to match each circumstance we meet, knowing that it will bring a constructive outcome.

So shall my word be that goes out from my mouth; it shall not return to me empty, but it shall accomplish that which I purpose, and shall succeed in the thing for which I sent it.
Isaiah 55:11

How then will they call on him in whom they have not believed? And how are they to believe in him of whom they have never heard? And how are they to hear without someone preaching?
Romans 10:14

Oh dear! There's that word "*preaching*"... I'm definitely not a preacher, so where does that leave me? Actually the original Greek word is κηρύσσοντος (*kēryssontos*) which means to announce, proclaim, or share a valuable message. For most of us that means just sharing personally in winsome words "*fitly spoken like apples of gold in a setting of silver*" that

24

reach right through to touch the hearts of those who hear them. Words like this flow freely when the Spirit of God has access to memory banks saturated with the Word of God.

Therefore, we are ambassadors for Christ, God making his appeal through us. We implore you on behalf of Christ, be reconciled to God. For our sake he made him to be sin who knew no sin, so that in him we might become the righteousness of God.
                                                                    2 Corinthians 5:20-21

If we will only do our part, which is to read, study, meditate and memorize His Word regularly, then we can count on His Spirit to summon up the words we need at the right time.

Trust in the LORD with all your heart, and do not lean on your own understanding. In all your ways acknowledge him, and he will make straight your paths.
                                                                    Proverbs 3:5-6

Now is the time to solidify a regular habit of daily Scripture reading, devotions, and journaling. If you haven't recently, please return to www.celebratesalvation.org/more and access the Stage A handouts that relate to daily devotions and Bible reading. Knowing, loving, and becoming immersed in the Word of God is one of the unmistakable marks of a true disciple.

My Study Habits and Methods

1. Have you been having any difficulty with getting established in a regular pattern of daily devotions and journaling?

2. How are you approaching studying the Scriptures? What could you do to improve your success and enjoyment?

3. Are you getting more comfortable with sharing the heart of God with others?

4. Do you have a prayer partner that you can communicate regularly with? How about your accountability partner?

5. Do you have a place in your journal where you can write down and reference Bible verses that are especially helpful to you?

Be thorough while you're answering each question by taking additional notes below as well as on additional sheets of paper or in an ongoing daily journal of your insights, meditations, prayers, and thoughts. Don't forget to memorize!

In this context you may enjoy reading our **The Art of Showing Up** handout, available online at www.celebratesalvation.org/more.

As we complete our first block of four lessons on our witness in **word**, guided by His Word, let us keep in mind the exhortation given to us by James, the brother of Jesus:

But be doers of the word, and not hearers only, deceiving yourselves. For if anyone is a hearer of the word and not a doer, he is like a man who looks intently at his natural face in a mirror. For he looks at himself and goes away and at once forgets what he was like. But the one who looks into the perfect law, the law of liberty, and perseveres, being no hearer who forgets but a doer who acts, he will be blessed in his doing. James 1:22-25

Lesson 5C
Recognizing the poor

Step 7: The Great Commission: Celebrate the joy of my salvation by following God's lead in bringing His Good News to others in word, **deed**, and power.

Recognizing those who are more likely to be broken, contrite, humble, and open about their neediness in our midst.

"Blessed are the poor in spirit, for theirs is the kingdom of heaven."

Matthew 5:3

And Jesus said to his disciples, "Truly, I say to you, only with difficulty will a rich person enter the kingdom of heaven."

Matthew 19:23

There are many dimensions to poverty, the simplest outline representing the three realms of human life: physical, psychological, and spiritual. We're more likely to think of the first two economic and psychosocial aspects which include financial, educational, cultural, vocational, and generational poverty. In His "world turned upside down" way, however, Jesus identifies riches as being an impediment and being *"poor in spirit"* as a blessing.

"Blessed are the meek, for they shall inherit the earth… the last will be first, and the first last."

Matthew 5:8, 20:16

What does it mean to be *"poor in spirit"*? The characteristics of this kind of "poverty" are humble contrition, awareness of need, and openness to assistance, correction, and instruction. Those who are full of themselves have no room for God and His Kingdom: they're the kings of their own kingdoms, lords of their own castles. It's much easier to identify with those who we think are poor when we recognize how poor we are ourselves.

The door to the Kingdom is closed to the proud but wide open to the *"poor in spirit"*. It's to these that we're called while we wait for the Holy Spirit to turn the hearts of others.

Sent: Becoming a Living Letter

Of course, there is another element to Jesus' call, which he announced in His hometown synagogue at Nazareth at the very onset of His ministry. Opening the scroll at Isaiah 61, He read,

"The Spirit of the Lord is upon me, because he has anointed me to proclaim good news to the poor. He has sent me to proclaim liberty to the captives and recovering of sight to the blind, to set at liberty those who are oppressed, to proclaim the year of the Lord's favor."
Luke 4:18-19

These are the ones who are open to the Gospel:

Listen, my beloved brothers, has not God chosen those who are poor in the world to be rich in faith and heirs of the kingdom, which he has promised to those who love him?
James 2:5

As you reach out to the people around you remember to guard against both pride and prejudice. Some who might look rich have emptied themselves and inwardly taken the form of servants, while others who appear to be poor are actually very resistant and full of themselves.

The bottom line: We need to avoid the trap of "toxic charity" by seeing people as Jesus sees them and then reaching out as He did to those who are genuinely poor and receptive.

My Awareness of Poverty

1. Do you think you are richer or poorer than other people? In what ways?

2. Who are some of the poor, captive, blind, or oppressed people in your life? Are you seeking relationships with any of them?

3. Are you and/or the church you attend located in proximity to those who might be hungry for the Gospel?

4. What does it mean to "preach to the choir"? How can you move outside your "comfort zone" to share with "the poor"?

Sent: Becoming a Living Letter

30

5. How do you think the Kingdom of God might favor those it counts to be poor?

Be thorough while you're answering each question by taking additional notes below as well as on additional sheets of paper or in an ongoing daily journal of your insights, meditations, prayers, and thoughts. Don't forget to memorize!

Lesson 6C
Opportunities to share

Step 7: The Great Commission: Celebrate the joy of my salvation by following God's lead in bringing His Good News to others in word, **deed**, and power.

What kind of ministries and situations are particularly likely to offer opportunities to share the Good News? How can you participate?

Let your first rule be: "Charity begins at home." This begs two definitions, what is "charity" and where is "home"? The Greek word underlying "charity" in the Bible is ἀγάπη (*agape*), which is divine, sacrificial love, as contrasted with simple affection and friendship. And "home" is where you live and includes who you live and work with plus all your neighbors. Start close and dive deep. This is what "loving your neighbor as yourself" is about.

Branching out from home (see **Note** on Page 34) is more likely to be successful if you've gotten practice close at hand first. If you can't get along with your family and neighbors, be careful about trying to do much better elsewhere, especially in situations where there may be cultural or language barriers.

There is also an ever-present and strong temptation to turn our attention to those that we consider to be less-fortunate than ourselves. We sympathize and want to help, so we offer to provide advice or food or clothing or money. Unfortunately, our well-intentioned efforts often have a paradoxically negative effect on both us and those we're trying to reach. The recipients can feel offended, patronized, or even entitled, while we may end up feeling used and unappreciated.

Taking this further, Robert Lupton advanced the following Oath for Compassionate Service in his book, *Toxic Charity*:

1. Never do for the poor what they have (or could have) the capacity to do for themselves.

Sent: Becoming a Living Letter

2. Limit one-way giving to emergency situations.

3. Strive to empower the poor through employment, lending, and investing, using grants sparingly to reinforce achievements.

4. Subordinate self-interests to the needs of those being served.

5. Listen closely to those you seek to help, especially to what is not being said – unspoken feelings may contain essential clues to effective service.

6. Above all, do no harm.

But let's take this a step further. What is the object? If your object is to share the Gospel with people, then the dominant word and concept should be "share." What can you do together that will cause a strong enough bond for the message of the Kingdom of God to come clearly through your words and actions?

Look for opportunities that embrace meeting felt needs with genuine mutuality, collaboration, and relationship, but also look for situations that include sharing in word as well as deed. Let the light of your hope so shine *"that they may see your good works... ask you for a reason for the hope that is in you... and give glory to your Father who is in heaven."*

(Matthew 5: 16 **and** 1 Peter 3:15)

My Ministry Ideas and Experiences

1. Can you remember any experiences with ministry that were particularly fruitful? How about ones that were discouraging?

2. What kind of talents and interests do you have that you think you would be especially good at sharing with others?

3. What could you and/or your family do with others in your neighborhood that would improve the quality of life there?

4. Does your church have any outreach activities that you and/or your family could participate in?

5. If you have children who are old enough to help out, what do you think you could do together with them?

Be thorough while you're answering each question by taking additional notes below as well as on additional sheets of paper or in an ongoing daily journal of your insights, meditations, prayers, and thoughts. Don't forget to memorize!

Lupton's full **Oath for Compassionate Service** is available as a handout at www.celebratesalvation.org/more. You may appreciate reading *Toxic Charity*, referenced on Page 60.

Note: Cross-cultural sharing falls into two categories, Short and Long Term. Immature believers can make positive contributions and receive great benefit from participating in well-organized Short Term missions. Long Term service (see Don Richardson's books on Page 60) generally requires much deeper maturity and preparation. Talk with your pastor about your aspirations.

Lesson 7C
Demonstrating God's love

Step 7: The Great Commission: Celebrate the joy of my salvation by following God's lead in bringing His Good News to others in word, **deed**, and power.

What are good ways to demonstrate the love of God?

You yourselves are our letter of recommendation, written on your hearts, to be known and read by all. And you show that you are a letter from Christ delivered by us, written not with ink but with the Spirit of the living God, not on tablets of stone but on tablets of human hearts. 2 Corinthians 3:2-3

Action, Attitude, and Availability

Action: As the folk proverb goes, "Actions speak louder than words." It's a part of the truth. Other corollaries might include "Don't offer unasked for advice (or help)" and "Talk is cheap." The Word of God is not cheap, however, and actions without any grateful references to your source of life may be mistaken for simple human kindness, which is good only as far as it goes.

Attitude: Avoid judging others, always remembering where you've come from and how He forgave you and set you free. Keep it down to earth and real. This is all about them, not you:

Do nothing from selfish ambition or conceit, but in humility count others more significant than yourselves. Philippians 2:3

Availability: If you're going to be there, be present 100% in body, soul, and spirit. Be accessible, approachable, open and accepting, empathetic and supportive. Major in encouragement and minor in instruction. Save correction for unusual circumstances.

Listen more than you talk. Get to know who people are and where they've come from. Become an expert at discovering the strengths of others. Rub people the right way so that you polish them and they shine.

Sent: Becoming a Living Letter

36

Smile often and laugh when it's appropriate, but be ready to weep when it gets real. *Let love be your aim*, as 1 Corinthians 14:1 counsels, and with practice you'll get closer and closer to hitting the mark consistently. Be kind to yourself and everyone around you: we're all in this together and only God Himself is perfect.

You may have gathered that the way we go about doing things is at least as important as what we actually do. Jesus identified Himself as *"the way, the truth, and the life."* We need to follow His way of love to demonstrate His truth and share His life effectively with others. Just as the tone of voice we use has to match our words, our attitude and approach have to match our actions or people on the receiving end may sense insincerity even if our hearts are pure.

All right, let's get practical. What can you do? Well, what do you know how to do best? Are there any skills or services you'd like to learn more about? What are your talents, abilities, and resources? We give out of the abundance of what we've been given and grow in knowledge and understanding along the way. Look for places to serve where God has already equipped you and go from there.

Look around your family, neighborhood, church, and job and see what God has prepared for you; pray about it; and then let the Holy Spirit guide and empower you along the way. As you abide in Him, He will flow through you, and fruit will be sure to come.

How I Can Share God's Love

1. Think about some times when a Christian brother or sister really helped you. How and what did they do that helped?

2. Are there times when you feel like giving someone a piece of your mind? How might God have you respond instead?

3. What are some interests that you would feel comfortable sharing in service with others?

4. Can you recall any negative experiences you've had in trying to share the love of God? Who do you think could coach you?

5. Can you think of anyone in your life that you've become alienated from? How might you reach across to them?

Be thorough while you're answering each question by taking additional notes below as well as on additional sheets of paper or in an ongoing daily journal of your insights, meditations, prayers, and thoughts. Don't forget to memorize!

This would also be a great time to review two of the handouts we mentioned in Lessons 3C and 4C, Charles Swindoll's well-known quote on **Attitude** and Rachel Wilkerson Miller's essay on **The Art of Showing Up**, both available at www.celebratesalvation.org/more.

Lesson 8C
Exercising our gifts

Step 7: The Great Commission: Celebrate the joy of my salvation by following God's lead in bringing His Good News to others in word, **deed**, and power.

What natural abilities, spiritual gifts, and calling have you been given and how can you seek to strengthen and use what you have so that you can receive more?

There are several kinds of gifts described in the Bible that are at work in our world. The words the Bible was written in can help. Gifts given to us by God include natural gifts (Greek δόματα or *domata*), which come with our heritage and upbringing, while spiritual gifts (Greek χαρίσματα or *charismata*) are imparted to us after we are drawn to Christ and born again by the gift (δωρεᾶς or *doreas*) of God's grace. In the Old Testament where spiritual gifts were less available, all of the above were included in the Hebrew term מַתָּן or *mattan*.

Then there are the gifts, presents, or offerings that we give to God and to others which are identified in NT Greek as δῶρόν (*dōron*) and in OT Hebrew as מִנְחָה (*minchah*).

The God-given gifts we received through inheritance (nature) and our environment (nurture) include our latent intelligence, physical strength and stamina, and human sensitivity as well as our abilities in language, athletics, mathematics, art, music, and vocational skills. By definition, gifts are given, not earned. As such, when we give our lives to Christ, we give Him back the *domata* he has given us to be used as *dōron* or *minchah* in His service.

The spiritual gifts or *charismata* are listed by Paul as follows:

Now there are varieties of gifts, but the same Spirit; and there are varieties of service, but the same LORD; and there are varieties of activities, but it is the same God who empowers them all in everyone. To each is given the manifestation of the Spirit for the common good. For to one is given through the Spirit the

Sent: Becoming a Living Letter

utterance of wisdom, and to another the utterance of knowledge according to the same Spirit, to another faith by the same Spirit, to another gifts of healing by the one Spirit, to another the working of miracles, to another prophecy, to another the ability to distinguish between spirits, to another various kinds of tongues, to another the interpretation of tongues. All these are empowered by one and the same Spirit, who apportions to each one individually as he wills.

1 Corinthians 12:4-11

A person may also have two kinds of callings, a "vocational" call to certain types of work and a "ministry" calling to certain roles of service and leadership in the Christian community. Usually the first are identified through interests and naturally developed abilities, while the second are discerned in concert with others only after someone has been born again into God's Kingdom.

Now you are the body of Christ and individually members of it. And God has appointed in the church first apostles, second prophets, third teachers, then miracles, then gifts of healing, helping, administrating, and various kinds of tongues. Are all apostles? Are all prophets? Are all teachers? Do all work miracles? Do all possess gifts of healing? Do all speak with tongues? Do all interpret? But earnestly desire the higher gifts.   1 Corinthians 12:27-31

Our part is to identify and exercise our gifts, be grateful and grow in them through practice, and earnestly seek all that He has for us.

Talents and Gifts

1. What natural gifts or talents do you have? Make a list and then gratefully turn them over to God one by one.

2. How do you think God might develop, redirect, or strengthen any of your natural abilities for Kingdom service?

3. What is your current vocation? Can you see yourself being used by God in this role? What other options do you see?

4. Have you received any spiritual gifts through prayer and the laying on of hands? What are they? Are you seeking more?

42

5. An old exercise mantra goes "use it or lose it." Are you using or practicing your gifts? Which ones, and how?

Be thorough while you're answering each question by taking additional notes below as well as on additional sheets of paper or in an ongoing daily journal of your insights, meditations, prayers, and thoughts. Don't forget to memorize!

Consider getting together with your pastor to discuss where you are in your growth as a believer with your spiritual gifts and calling.

Lesson 9C
Natural and supernatural

Step 7: The Great Commission: Celebrate the joy of my salvation by following God's lead in bringing His Good News to others in word, deed, and **power**.

How does God still move in power to confirm His presence? What is truly natural *vs.* supernatural? The miracle of salvation and healing in today's world.

To what degree do salvation and healing of any kind require supernatural intervention? Just think about it. Is it possible for anyone to be saved apart from God's active participation? What about healing in a world where everything seems to deteriorate when left to its own devices? Clearly, God's supernatural grace is at work in both of these processes.

With physical healing, we often try to distinguish between what might appear to be natural and the miraculous by how long it takes for a condition to be healed – long for natural and shorter for miraculous. Where, if anywhere, is the cutoff? Considerations like these can help reveal the supernatural activity that is at work underlying the continuum of healing.

Paul presents a different dichotomy in 1 Corinthians 12: 29-30: *Do all work miracles? Do all possess gifts of healing?* which would suggest that some miracles may be distinguished from the more blended experience of healing. However, both are evidences of God's active grace, making the distinction more one of whether we are dealing with "common" or "uncommon" (amazing) grace. We tend to take note of "miracles" but take "healing" for granted unless there is something about it that seems uncommon to us.

Let's compare two other situations: the parable of the Good Samaritan and Jesus' Great Commission. Both were commended by God and required His grace to accomplish. The Good Samaritan was actually presented as a member of a despised neighboring culture of

44

unbelievers. He was given as an example of someone who, by common grace without even a profession of faith, could "love his neighbor" in an admirable way.

The Great Commission, however, requires calling, consecration, giftedness, and a level of focused faith that is able to work together with God to demonstrate His amazing grace.

And he said to them, "Go into all the world and proclaim the gospel to the whole creation. Whoever believes and is baptized will be saved, but whoever does not believe will be condemned. And these signs will accompany those who believe: in my name they will cast out demons; they will speak in new tongues; they will pick up serpents with their hands; and if they drink any deadly poison, it will not hurt them; they will lay their hands on the sick, and they will recover."

Mark 16:15-18

Hold on a moment. Let's step aside briefly from some of the more difficult portions of this passage that talk about demons, serpents, and poison while we go further into learning what's involved in being vessels of God's grace as new believers. The Great Commission clearly anticipates the availability and exercise of God's gifts of love and power to strengthen our witness as we share the Gospel message. How can we best cooperate with Him?

My Awareness of the Supernatural

1. Can you recall any times in your life when it seemed that God was "showing up" in a palpable way? What happened?

2. Have you or anyone you know experienced a miracle or healing in answer to prayer? How about your own salvation?

3. List some possible ways that God could demonstrate His love and power through the active witness of a committed believer.

4. Do you have any examples of times in your life when God answered your prayer or witness with clear evidence?

5. Which gifts of the Spirit have you experienced in your life so far, and which ones are you seeking now?

Be thorough while you're answering each question by taking additional notes below as well as on additional sheets of paper or in an ongoing daily journal of your insights, meditations, prayers, and thoughts. Don't forget to memorize!

You may appreciate **Biblical Words for Power**, a handout available at www.celebratesalvation.org/more.

Lesson 10C
Seeking God for the afflicted

Step 7: The Great Commission: Celebrate the joy of my salvation by following God's lead in bringing His Good News to others in word, deed, and **power**.

Seeking God's presence and power on behalf of those who are afflicted.

How do we go about becoming channels of God's supernatural grace and power, especially as we reach out with compassion to those who are afflicted around us?

What characteristics does a wire have to have to be able to carry a heavy charge of high voltage electricity? Well, first it has to be pure, strong, and completely free of any tendency to divert the power to its own ends. Any attempt to take hold of the flow of power will end up in burnout and loss of the wire. God will not charge us with more of His power than we can handle, so He limits how much He shares to our ability to let it pass through.

The index of our ability to let Him flow is not only in how many gifts of the Spirit we've received but in how much of the fruit of the Holy Spirit we've allowed Him to produce in us as we abide in the Vine (see John 15). Let's list the fruit again:

*But the fruit of the Spirit is (1) **love**, (2) **joy**, (3) **peace**, patience, kindness, goodness, faithfulness, gentleness, self-control; against such things there is no law.*

Galatians 5:22-23

You can be assured that bearing good fruit will not only increase your compassion but prevent burn out. As Peter elaborated:

For this very reason, make every effort to supplement your faith with virtue, and virtue with knowledge, and knowledge with self-control, and self-control with steadfastness, and steadfastness with godliness, and godliness with brotherly affection, and brotherly affection with love. For if these qualities are yours and are increasing, they keep you from being ineffective or unfruitful in the knowledge of our Lord Jesus Christ. 2 Peter 1:5-8

Another Scriptural guide is the example of others who have demonstrated God's grace, love and power in their lives. Start with Jesus Himself and follow up with the apostles and disciples noted in the Book of Acts. You may also, as a born-again believer who is being cleansed (sanctified = becoming a saint), appreciate studying the lives of noteworthy "saints" who have gone before.

Let's put things in priority order:

1) *Pursue **love**, and earnestly desire the spiritual gifts, especially that you may prophesy... the one who prophesies speaks to people for their upbuilding and encouragement and consolation.* 1 Corinthians 12:1, 3

2) *The **joy** of the Lord is your strength.* Nehemiah 8:10

3) *And the **peace** of God, which surpasses all understanding, will guard your hearts and your minds in Christ Jesus.* Philippians 4:7

Then keep going. Allow the vinedresser to nurture, prune, and water you. The fruit comes as a matter of course as the sap flows freely from the root out to the tips of each branch. Just let go, grow, and let God do the work in and through you.

My Desire for His Fruit and Gifts

1. How do you think you're doing in manifesting the fruit of the Spirit in your life? List your growth priorities below:

2. Have there been any times when people tried to minister to you when you were doubtful about their love for you?

3. Scriptures say a lot about "patience" (or "longsuffering"). What does this say about God's way of loving the afflicted?

4. What do you think of when the gifts of prophesy and healing are mentioned? What does the Bible say about these gifts?

50

5. As you study about the gifts of the Holy Spirit, which ones do you have questions about? Who can you ask?

Be thorough while you're answering each question by taking additional notes below as well as on additional sheets of paper or in an ongoing daily journal of your insights, meditations, prayers, and thoughts. Don't forget to memorize!

You may also appreciate **Two Manifestations of Grace**, a handout available at www.celebratesalvation.org/more.

Lesson 11C
Salvation and healing

Step 7: The Great Commission: Celebrate the joy of my salvation by following God's lead in bringing His Good News to others in word, deed, and **power**.

Praying for salvation and healing for others and then following up.

Our world is full of two things: suffering and grace. Sometimes we seem to be "going from pillar to post" or, as the old saying goes, "If it isn't one thing, it's another." When we look around and count our blessings, however, we can step aside from our own trials far enough to empathize with others who are going through difficult times. We've been there in one way or another whether it's the result of our own sin or just the trials of life. Remember, we're serving on the "grace" side with One who understands:

For we do not have a high priest who is unable to sympathize with our weaknesses, but one who in every respect has been tempted as we are, yet without sin. Hebrews 4:15

Our first impulse should be to intercede before God in prayer, seeking relief on behalf of those who are suffering and wisdom about how we can help. Good Samaritan grace is never out of style. James offers the following guidance for us all:

Is anyone among you suffering? Let him pray. Is anyone cheerful? Let him sing praise. Is anyone among you sick? Let him call for the elders of the church, and let them pray over him, anointing him with oil in the name of the Lord. And the prayer of faith will save the one who is sick, and the Lord will raise him up. And if he has committed sins, he will be forgiven.

*Therefore, confess your sins to one another and pray for one another, that you may be healed. The prayer of a righteous person has **great power** as it is working. Elijah was a man with a nature like ours, and he prayed fervently that it might not rain, and for three years and six months it did not rain on the earth. Then he prayed again, and heaven gave rain, and the earth bore its fruit.*

Sent: Becoming a Living Letter

My brothers, if anyone among you wanders from the truth and someone brings him back, let him know that whoever brings back a sinner from his wandering will save his soul from death and will cover a multitude of sins.

James 5:13-20

How do we pray? Start by seeking God's face for a clear revelation of His will in the situation, followed by a confirming inner witness. With practice comes mature discernment and confidence that our prayers will be answered as we have offered them.

And this is the confidence that we have toward him, that if we ask anything according to his will he hears us. And if we know that he hears us in whatever we ask, we know that we have the requests that we have asked of him.

1 John 5:14-15

Then what? Pray, let go and let God guide you, and then follow up. "Ask and keep on asking; seek and keep on seeking; knock and keep on knocking." Keep on and keep up with confidence that He who hears will continue to comfort, guide, reveal, and strengthen.

Rejoice always; pray without ceasing; give thanks in all circumstances for this is the will of God in Christ Jesus for you.

1 Thessalonians 5:16-18

My Intercessory Life

1. Do you know someone who is going through a hard time? What would be some good ways to reach out to them?

2. Is prayer an episodic event or an ongoing relationship with God for you? How do you see yourself growing in prayer?

3. How do you hope others will respond when you are suffering? Do you follow the guidance James has offered?

4. How do you handle it when answers to your prayers seem to be absent or delayed?

54

5. James speaks of the great power our prayers can have. How can you cooperate with God in releasing His power in prayer?

Be thorough while you're answering each question by taking additional notes below as well as on additional sheets of paper or in an ongoing daily journal of your insights, meditations, prayers, and thoughts. Don't forget to memorize!

Lesson 12C
Imparting the gifts

Step 7: The Great Commission: Celebrate the joy of my salvation by following God's lead in bringing His Good News to others in word, deed, and **power**.

God's gifts imparted and power applied in prayer with the laying on of hands.

Many new believers somehow receive the mistaken impression that the exercise of the gifts of the Holy Spirit should be sudden and dramatic. While it's true that the gift of tongues often manifests itself soon after receiving the baptism in the Holy Spirit, the other gifts not only take time to develop but may be less visible or only operate infrequently.

The primary fruit that's necessary to allow the gifts room to operate is patience – waiting and quietly staying available.

And let us not grow weary of doing good, for in due season we will reap, if we do not give up.
Galatians 6:9

He gives power to the faint, and to him who has no might he increases strength. Even youths shall faint and be weary, and young men shall fall exhausted; but they who wait for the Lord shall renew their strength; they shall mount up with wings like eagles; they shall run and not be weary; they shall walk and not faint.
Isaiah 40:29-31

The terminology that Isaiah used refers to this reality. It often takes time for God's grace to work because He's accomplishing many things as time elapses. We also aren't the only ones who are waiting: God waits for us far more than we wait for Him.

The Lord is not slow to fulfill his promise as some count slowness, but is patient toward you, not wishing that any should perish, but that all should reach repentance.
2 Peter 3:9

How long does He wait before we say "yes" to Him when He calls? What does He need to get lined up before He can do the next step?

Sent: Becoming a Living Letter

Who needs to be in the right place at the right time for His will to be accomplished while He keeps all of our free wills intact?

And what does this have to do with our topic? It's actually quite simple. You can't just run up to somebody without asking, lay your hands on them, let loose with prayer, and expect to see miraculous results worked by God's power. He's the Ultimate Gentleman.

People need to be open to prayer from you and ready to receive the flow of His grace, while you need to hear from God that this is the time and place. It's always best to seek and receive permission not only to pray with and for someone but to touch them. Prayer with the laying on of hands is an experience that often has life-changing consequences.

Similar to the way medical providers obtain informed consent, you briefly inform the person about what you're proposing to do and the intended consequences as well as what might happen differently. Another medical similarity is to remain humble as you remember that you're still "practicing" spiritual care. Then be bold, gentle, and proceed with confidence that God is with you:

As each has received a gift, use it to serve one another, as good stewards of God's varied grace.
                                        1 Peter 4:10

My Role in Imparting His Power

1. It's said that "practice makes perfect" but missteps may come along the way. What experiences with prayer have you had?

2. Trial and error also go with "if at first you don't succeed, try, try again." Have you turned any prayer errors into successes?

3. How do you think your Heavenly Father views your sincere mistakes? Would He rather have you hold back or go ahead?

4. What would you like God to show and teach you about this whole topic of exercising spiritual gifts? Make a short list here.

Sent: Becoming a Living Letter

5. What plans do you have on your heart for continuing your spiritual growth as a disciple of Jesus?

Be thorough while you're answering each question by taking additional notes below as well as on additional sheets of paper or in an ongoing daily journal of your insights, meditations, prayers, and thoughts. Don't forget to keep up your daily devotions and Scripture memorization!

As you come to the close of our discipleship course, you may enjoy reading an introduction to Bob Sorge's devotional guide on *Secrets of the Secret Place* called **Chapter 50 of Sorge's** *Secrets*, available as a handout at www.celebratesalvation.org/more. Information about his full book is listed there as well as on Page 60 among the Suggestions for Further Study. Additional study materials and video messages are available to accompany Sorge's book. Check online for availability of further books in the *Joy of Christian Discipleship Series*.

Commendation

Congratulations! After learning about the riches of your salvation and the wonderful life-long process of sanctification and discipleship, you've just completed our study of what it is to be sent as His ambassadors to a broken and fallen world.

Let's keep it up together with God as we participate actively in His loving plan not only to make our lives whole but to keep them that way by cleansing, purifying, enriching, and empowering us so that we can live, touch other lives, and keep on bearing fruit in every good work. Find your gifts and place in the Body of Christ and in a local church fellowship (see our handout on **Expressions of Christianity**) as you continue to apply yourself to Scripture study, prayer, journaling, fellowship, and growing in faith as a joyful disciple of the living God.

For this reason, because I have heard of your faith in the Lord Jesus and your love toward all the saints, I do not cease to give thanks for you, remembering you in my prayers, that the God of our Lord Jesus Christ, the Father of glory, may give you the Spirit of wisdom and of revelation in the knowledge of him, having the eyes of your hearts enlightened, that you may know what is the hope to which he has called you, what are the riches of his glorious inheritance in the saints, and what is the immeasurable greatness of his power toward us who believe, according to the working of his great might. Ephesians 1:15-19

May our Lord and Savior continue to bless, favor, encourage, sanctify, and send you forth for service in His Kingdom!

Suggestions for Further Study

The Holy Bible
English Standard Version® ESV Study Bible™.

James Choung and **Ryan Pfeiffer**
Longing for Revival: Holy Discontent to Breakthrough Faith.

Martin Luther King, Jr.
Strength to Love and *Where Do We Go From Here - Chaos or Community?*

George E. Ladd
The Gospel of the Kingdom.

C. S. Lewis
How to Be a Christian and *Miracles.*

Robert Lupton
Toxic Charity: How Churches/Charities Hurt Those They Help

John M. Perkins
Dream with Me: Race, Love, and *The Struggle We Must Win.*

Don Richardson
Peace Child and *Eternity in Their Hearts.*

Bob Sorge
Secrets of the Secret Place: Igniting Your Personal Time with God.

Dallas Willard
The Divine Conspiracy: Rediscovering Our Hidden Life in God.

Additional Celebrate Salvation® Resources

Books in the Joy of Christian Discipleship Series

The Joy of Christian Discipleship Course 1
Established in 3 Stages and 7 Steps, a 36-week group study

1. **Stage A – Saved!** *Rescued by Grace*

2. **Stage B – Sanctified:** *Coming Clean with God*

3. **Stage C – Sent:** *Becoming a Living Letter* (this book)
   Stage C Handouts *
   Good News in The Lord's Prayer (1C)
   God Governs in Mankind's Affairs (2C)
   Attitude – Charles Swindoll (3C)
   The Art of Showing Up (4C)
   Oath for Compassionate Service (6C)
   Biblical Words for Power (9C)
   Two Manifestations of Grace (10C)
   Chapter 50 of Sorge's *Secrets* (12C)
   Expressions of Christianity
   Plus – Handouts and Worksheets or **Complete Course 1**

Devotional Guide to 3 Stages and 7 Steps *
4. **Essentials of the Christian Faith**
   7 Steps to Abundant Life, an 8-week daily devotional guide

The Joy of Christian Discipleship Course 2 *
Equipped with Understanding, a 36-week group study

5. **Awakening:** *The Triumph of Truth*

6. **Kingdom:** *God's Reign in our Midst*

7. **Heaven:** *Our Ultimate Destiny*

   Plus – Handouts and Worksheets or **Complete Course 2**

* Links to all handouts in printable PDF form as well as suggested books and information about Additional Resources can be found online at www.celebratesalvation.org/more. Books 4-7 are under development at the time of this publication.